A TIME OF MIRACLES

Adapted by Eva Moore

an imprint of

SCHOLASTIC INC.

New York Toronto London Auckland Sydney
Mexico City New Delhi Hong Kong Buenos Aires

ISBN 0-439-85879-8

12 11 10 9 8 7 6 5 4 3 2 1 6 7 8 9 10 11/0

Illustrations by Duendes del Sur
Designed by Joan Moloney

Printed in the U.S.A.
First printing, October 2006

EDUCATOR'S NOTE

Stories from the Gospels

Dear Parents,

Welcome to the Scholastic Read and Learn Bible Readers series. We have more than 80 years of experience with teachers, parents, and children and put it into a program that is designed to match your child's interests and skills.

- Look at the book together. Encourage your child to read the title and make a prediction about the story.

- Read the book together. Encourage your child to sound out words when appropriate. When your child struggles, you can help by providing the word.

- Encourage your child to retell the story. This is a great way to check for comprehension.

Scholastic Readers are designed to support your child's efforts to learn how to read at every age and every stage. Enjoy helping your child learn to read and love to read.

—Francie Alexander
Chief Academic Officer
Scholastic Inc.

God sent an angel to earth, an angel named Gabriel.

Gabriel went to the city of Jerusalem. An old man named Zechariah lived there. When Zechariah saw the angel, he couldn't believe his eyes.

“Don’t be afraid,” Gabriel said. “I am a servant of the Lord God, and I have good news to tell you.”

"God has found favor with you. He is giving you a son. You will call him John. John will do great work for the Lord."

Zechariah and his wife, Elizabeth, had always wanted a child. They were very happy.

Then Gabriel went to the town of Nazareth. He found a young woman named Mary. He had a message for her, too.

“God has blessed you,” Gabriel told Mary. “You will have a son. His name will be Jesus. He will be great, and one day people will call him Son of God Most High.”

A few months later, Zechariah's wife, Elizabeth, had a baby boy, just as Gabriel had said. He was named John.

Then it was time for Mary's baby to be born. Mary and her husband, Joseph, were in the town of Bethlehem, many miles from home. The city was crowded, and they couldn't find a room at the inn.

Their baby, Jesus, was born in a stable.
That very night, a bright star shone in the sky.

Some shepherds saw the star. Then angels appeared to them. The angels told them about a special baby that had just been born in Bethlehem. This baby was born to be their Savior. They said he was Christ the Lord.

The shepherds went to Bethlehem. They found the baby Jesus lying in a manger of hay. They went down on their knees to thank God.

Later, some kings from the East arrived in Bethlehem. They had followed the star to see the baby. They gave him precious gifts. They knew he was to be the King of Kings.

Many years passed.

Jesus lived in Nazareth with his parents, Mary and Joseph.

He became a carpenter, like his father. He seemed to be an ordinary man.

The boy John grew up, too. But he did not seem ordinary. John lived alone in the desert. He wore a tunic of scratchy camel's hair. He ate whatever food he could find in the desert, even grasshoppers.

God had sent him to make the people ready for their Savior, Jesus.

God told John to go to the valley of the Jordan River.

John stood by the river and called to the people who passed by.

"Turn back to God. Come into the river with me. God will wash away your sins and you will be happy."

John's words gave people great hope.

Crowds came to the river to be baptized and have their sins washed away.

John told them God wanted them to think of others.

"If you have two coats and you see someone with none, give that person one of yours. If you have food, share it with someone who is hungry."

People began to say that John must be the Savior whose coming had been expected for hundreds of years.

But John said, "No, I am not the one you have been waiting for. He is coming soon. I am not good enough even to untie his sandals."

One day when John was baptizing people in the Jordan River, a man came and stood on the riverbank. He seemed like an ordinary man. But John knew he was not ordinary. He was Jesus, the true Savior.

Jesus asked John to baptize him.

John thought it should be the other way around. "I should be baptized by you," he said to Jesus. But Jesus said that this was what God wanted them to do.

So John baptized Jesus in the Jordan River.

Afterward, Jesus prayed. A bright light filled the sky and the Holy Spirit came down upon him. It looked like a dove.

A voice from Heaven said, "You are My own dear Son, and I am pleased with you."

And so it all came to pass as the angel Gabriel had said. John the Baptist had led the way for Jesus, and Jesus led the people in the way of God.

He was called the Son of God Most High.

Did you know . . .

Page 4

. . . that Jerusalem is one of the oldest continuously inhabited cities in the world? There is evidence that people have lived in Jerusalem for more than 4,000 years.

Page 7

. . . that Nazareth is a town in what was the Roman province of Galilee?

Page 11

. . . that Bethlehem was also the birthplace of King David?

Page 13

. . . that a savior is one who rescues or sets people free?

Page 15

. . . that the three kings from the East were called the Magi?

Pages 18-19

. . . that John probably lived in the desert of Judea, which is between Jerusalem and the Dead Sea?

Pages 20-21

. . . that baptism symbolizes the washing away of sins and the start of a renewed life?

Page 28-29

. . . that the Holy Spirit gives people the ability to understand God's will, to live together in peace, and to be obedient to God?